POEMS

THE MOUNTAIN THAT EATS MEN
AARON ERICKSEN

JALAPEÑO PUBLISHING
COLLEGE PARK, MARYLAND

Published by Jalapeño Publishing
www.jalapenopublishing.com
Copyright © 2019 Aaron Ericksen
All rights reserved
Manufactured in the United States of America

An Jalapeño Publishing Original
FIRST PRINTING

Editor: Brittany Micka-Foos
Artwork: Marion Ericksen
Typeface: Bembo, Chantelli Antiqua

LIBRARY OF CONGRESS CATALOGING IN PUBLICATION DATA
Ericksen, Aaron 1957–
    The mountain that eats men: poems / Aaron Ericksen
    ISBN ISBN-13: 978-0-9983614-5-1

Acknowledgements

The author wishes to thank his family for their love, support, and inspiration. A very special thanks to Brittany Micka-Foos for her insights and patience while editing. Thanks to my publisher and wife Oksana; without your love and unwavering support these poems would disappear in the vapors of my mind.

A special acknowledgement goes to M. Dale Kinkade who was a linguist with expertise in the Salish languages. He conducted field work on several severely endangered languages, including the Upper Chehalis, which served as one voice for the poem Confluence.

This book is dedicated to my father who taught me to love the land and my mother who showed me how to see it.

Contents

In Memory

Confluence

Waterfall

The Weathering

Alberobello

Coordinates: 724, 730, 4612, 4615, 13

Dark Shadows

Stitches of Melancholia

Prepositions

Three Deadly Words

Terra Nova in Tirana

North Ontario

Apples in Zhongguancun

The Ragpicker's Dream

The Mountain That Eats Men

The notion that all these fragments are separately existent is evidently an illusion, and this illusion cannot do other than lead to endless conflict and confusion.

—David Bohm

In Memory

We lift ourselves
From the darkness of our shadows

We consume our future
On the wings of sparrows

Our reflections shimmer
When our voices become wordless

A pair of eyes
Recall the innocence

A priestly hand
Transmutes the dream

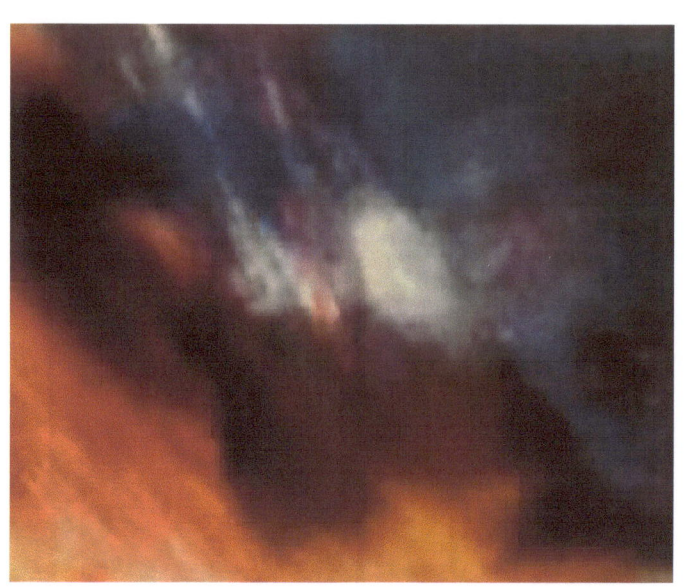

Confluence [1]

I don't believe in magic. I believe in the sun and the stars, the water, the tides, the floods, the owls, the hawks flying, the river running, the wind talking. They're measurements. They tell us how healthy things are. How healthy we are.

Because we and they are the same.

—Billy Frank

The land trades stories with us
if we share our stories, it keeps them.
There is an ancient reciprocity
between us and the eyes of the world.
In this tradition, it is how the land multiplies witness
to the length of our own lives
and what we might gain
by listening to our world.
That is the topic of this tale.

Like a river flowing, my mind retreats:
wind whistling through an old '49 Chevy
bouncing down highway ninety-nine
past Tumwater, Maytown, Little Rock   *il wyanits'*
into the forested Black Hills
where Muskrat Mountain   *masilc'Jscwa*
cast a westerly shadow
over an old circus tent father pitched
on the bank of Waddle Creek.   *tsa'.pc*

Where tsa'.pc started, no one knows   *Waddle Creek*
like dreams revisited in twilight
sacred is the source
awakening in morning shadows.
Better to follow where dreams and creeks flow
meandering many vales through dark woods
lined with bracken fern   *patakwn'l*
where spirit-power parcels innocence   *tunaqinl*
into a place of confluence.

To where pools reside in deep pockets of stone — *spataɬ*
lurking among the rocky shelves.
To where tsa'.pc embraces the Black River — *Waddle Creek embraces sacel'l*
dancing waters drum and sing, comingling
as if they'd always known each other.
Maybe they had —
maybe they had the same source
a source so deeply buried — *masilc'I scwa*
that you could not find it
by looking for it.

In the long hot summer of '85
I revisited tsa'.pc. — *Waddle Creek*
Strolling at night by the old stream
as she struggled to survive
exhausted, falling shallow — *sxwi*
a few steps from the conflux,
her few remaining rivulets descending — *lixw*
into the world of the dead. — *ʔalk'wt*

The ribald trickster — *kwoh-neh*
stranded minnows — *snewms'*
      and crawfish — *sc'al'x̱*
in a cul-de-sac a few yards from sacel'l. — *Black River*
Gone the Oregon white oak
once guarding our camp,
gone many ash trees — *tawasaʔintums*
that bent toward river's bank,
gone the huckleberry — *st'exwɬn'*
    salmonberry   *yetwaʔ*
        gooseberry   *t'amexwn'l*
            and red-flowering currant   *p'uqwaʔ*
replaced by a rusty mobile home
where our old gray tent once stood.

The last active speaker of the Kwaiailk [2]
died in the shadow of the Black Hills in 2001.
Where did his language go?
From what source can it be silenced?
Does it speak still,
from the terrain that once bore witness
to the land of healing rain?   *xasil'*
Should I be surprised
when the creeks cry out,
speaking truth
in the silence of the wood?

Between sleep and waking life
burns a lingering dream: *xasipl̓ixw*
tsa'.pc and sacel'l meet again   *Waddle Creek and Black River*
near Mima Mounds prairie   *nsq'wanx̣[tn*
a holy burial place.   *xaxa.ʔ mak'wtn'l*
Their bodies gently comingle
quietly invoking a language now lost
to a world of ghosts.   *sk'eyaxasms*

Then, as if they had nowhere in particular to go,
as darkness falls, they slipped away
toward the sunset, toward the ocean   *sla*
from a world that was dying.

[1] Source for Upper Chehalis words: Kinkade, M. Dale (1963). Phonology and Morphology of Upper Chehalis: I. International Journal of American Linguistics.

[2] For many centuries, the Chehalis people or Tsihalis lived along the Chehalis River which had as one of its tributaries the Black River. The Upper Chehalis (Q̓ʷay̓ áyiɬq or Kwaiailk) spoke Tsamosan, a distinct member of the Coast Salish family of Salishan languages.

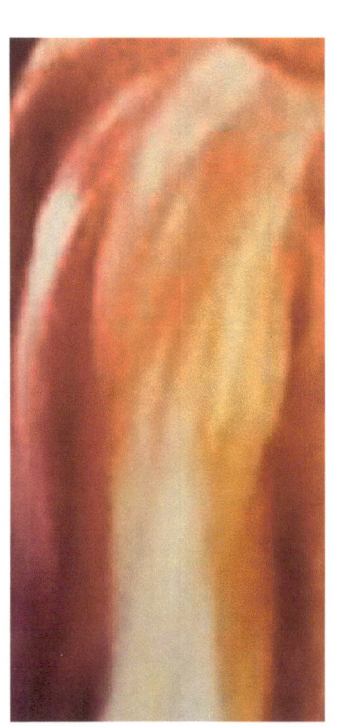

Waterfall

Waterfall
birthed in the wild
where once healing spirits
thundered through earth's
retreating mountains
shaking the edges
of falling hope

Are you dying, while I'm dancing
navigating alone in madness?

Can you count on me to ease your painful
rhythms on this droughtful day?

Are we singing
into endless waterfalls
spilling over obligations
of ancestral alters
moving desert spirits
who pass this way
weeping?

The Weathering

Beyond a critical point within a finite space, freedom diminishes as numbers increase.
—Pardot Kynes, the "First Planetologist of Arrakis"

A lone wolf lies hidden
among lichened rocks
conquering earth's crust
detrited and chafed
bits of time
marking the years
and the decline of life.

A weeping downpour
washes lichen from basalt
down blue mountain
meandering dense hemlock
deep into Buckhorn Wilderness
where lichen feed
a lush green valley
between Turbal Cain and Marmot Pass,
domus to Roosevelt elk
grazing on fen-sedges and ferns
cattails, bear grass, sweet grass,
and plant roots
Elwa once used
to weave baskets and mats
from which to sit
and bear witness
to lagom
rain
      river
            renewal

Can Palantir encode this experience?

Far from the deserts
and wastelands
the dawning
of a new microcosm emerges
far from earth's
sloth
        habits
                waste

SpaceX delivers pay-to-play
Oscar Wilde's cynics,
gluttonous oligarchs,
and president's heirs
seek new trophies
for their garish towers.
Squint closely now
between lines of vision and blurring
high upon Blue Mountain
a lone wolf lies hidden.
Down below,
newly minted Roosevelt Elk
await slaughter
as the mighty slayer
questions the Avatar:
was this truly the way it was?

        Stop!

        Start all over again.

We've been waiting
for a guide to take us
to where a lone wolf lies hidden
among lichened rocks.
Sit quiet now
on the colored floor
a meadow,
its lighted ceiling
a morning sky,
and listen
to the witnesses
whispering
down from sacred mountains
through dense hemlock and cedar.
Don't forget the lichen,
it has an uncanny ability
to detect
          pollution.

Apples in Zhongguancun

simple fluency eludes
network blind leaders
puzzles frack their world

dangers are disconnected
problems linger on fractured bases
marking cracks growing over time

potential threats, reduced to nouns
switches, chips, data, code
become threats potential

trapped in the years
the Colonels liberate their daughters
into a world of databases

for all our Crosby's
it is the end of everything
every cupboard, flagstone, chair, and table

and now we are going off, alone
lamenting the decline of tv and newspapers
a disconnected age

we are now connected
through our apps of the moment
whence the sharpest edges rise
from relationships

hold vivid, the picture dear
of roads, rivers, and mountain ranges
networked canals in the Yucatan
without losing sense of your surroundings

a world of constant connection
lashing us into addled masses
to be fought, manipulated, and braced against
for what need is there for liberty or fairness?

God forbid, programming is Tantalus
tempting to peddle
to investors, technocrats, and politicians
a near total lack of diversity

let the machines do it
the price of meshing
our hopes and hatreds
will be too high a bitcoin

The Ragpicker's Dream

The old man stoops
and fans the flies with his hand
back bent, wrinkled neck extended
like an ancient brown tortoise.
His ragged shirt
gives less protection than a shell
from the searing sun
that scorched the forests
from Greece to Paradise
that year.

Behind him, a wall
surrounding the American Villa
where diplomats look down upon Tirana
from carpeted lawns
and ornamented living rooms,
ordained with Balkan souvenirs.
Before him the refuse
of last night's party,
lifting a small plastic bottle
to his lips
wiping his brow, before drinking
murmuring the ragpicker's dream
fat i mirë është imi—good fortune is mine.

In the center
of the same city
at that very moment
the Albanian Minister of Economic Development
was thinking the same thing
as he raised a crystal glass
at the five-star hotel
to toast Nestle's
water rights purchase.
One of the two was mistaken.

Coordinates: 724, 730, 4612, 4615, 13

How long since I wrote
a simple song, at least
it's been two years.

Gone the timing
the rhyming, the palette of words
that moved like brush strokes alla prima.

I lost everything that once birthed
unwitting inner perspective
for which to see the virgin canvas.

Where shall I turn?

To the moon?
Wandering in midnight blue,
silent weariness descending.

To the tides?
Contours rising, as twilight darkens
double shadows to remind me.

To the mask?
Projecting in a contoured mirror
diffuse figures of light.

You who painted middle ground
before Ana Mendieta
intersected identities with Niles Born.

You who rendered vast panorama,
glazed the caress of a breeze
emanating from anxious noisy streets.

I shall look to the stars
a Silueta Series rippling sublime
punctuating the vast stillness
so that your art will never die.

                        To Marion Alice Armstrong

Alberobello

That signature,
       T. Matsujima

at the bottom right
of the canvas
in its customary home

surrounded
by chromatic black foreground
underlying dense
concentrations of trulli

those timeless Apulian
dry stone huts
with their conical
limestone slab roofs

I don't know why
that reminded me
of your features
appearing forty-seven years
after the fact
comforting me

your kindly presence
didn't look at me
rather looking ahead
as we drove from my high school
down Sleater-Kinney
to St. Peters
to see my father
lying with tubes
that fed
a broken heart

and I looked at you,
as I looked away from him
and realized you were more
than a football coach
disinterested in skinny freshmen
who couldn't pass
or catch
unless your best friend could
and that was good enough
when you were looking at me

in the exalted night of Alberobello,
beneath
a soundless rain
tapping trulli roofs
I dreamed of you
and thanked
   T. Matsujima

Dark Shadows

Glass shatters near midnight
the vampire exits to the dawn
leaving scars that will last
forever

Waltzing cataleptic on the lawn
his wailing covers me
repeating in my dreams
cacophony

Blood seeps from wounds
friends could see but never touch
yet, with faith venomous,
i believed

Dreams of pigs on the ceiling
Somnambulists cast
radiating cold shards of broken glass
Ha-ha charade you are

Dreams of one
lone maple in the bracken
where innocence,
not lost but taken
festered ever darkening
forests of isolation

Isn't this where?

In my fear of becoming
a creature of the night
I kept our secret behind a wall

In my fear of regenerating
I lose touch with the day
to protect the ecclesiastical

In my fear I escaped to prison
where other wounded souls
slew all that they hated
with crimson stakes to bare

Wandering down vacuous streets
eternal nights, in search of Proserpine
resting weary arms in empty vessels
until the sun shines on high

Will this chiaroscuro world end
in the sun or in the shade?
When ... will my soul have its day?

Smile, my brother, in your slumber
you may yet wake
to find the dawning of the day

I, however, will sleepwalk nights
amidst stars coldly blinking
till dark shadows rise in morning's tears.

Stitches of Melancholia

Charlie, Willie, and Lewis—
Border Scot descendants
from the debatable lands
wedged between Marshall Meadows Bay
and the Solway Firth,
a realm of mixed allegiances
where clans switched loyalty
as suited their needs on any given day—
settled in the Highlands
just outside Battleground,
ironically named after a battle
that never happened
between the messianic
and a Sahaptian tribe
who dared to resist
moving to the rez, far
from the debatable lands.

One boyish morning
Charlie pranked poor brother Lew
sitting down to ham and eggs
minus the ham and the chair.
Charlie and Lewis never spoke again
nary a treaty nor reunion.
I saw Uncle Lewis once
when i was ten
long after Charlie died,
his crumpled shadow slinking
from Uncle Willie's porch,
the screen door slamming away
the early morning melancholic vapors.

★★★★

Borgvald, master accountant
adept at quantifying
paper boxes to be shipped
in orderly fashion,
all relationships must square,
no deviance from the norm,
even fortifying a contract
for the valuation and vagaries
of marriage.

Parents don't behave accordingly?
Amortize the assets!
Friends stray from the plan?
Subtract them from the ledger!
With a hard-edged gaze
he found Charlie's depression
a galling liability—
no reconciliation in store
just a simple write off.

However, melancholia doesn't add up
no single entry explains
life in the red.

★★★★

Mary Mad Queen
adept at strip-mining
banished the minions
before their time,
the quiet ones, odd ones
idiosyncratic ones,
with stains on their ties
who dared to march
against the grain.

Out to pasture,
grazing out their days
in the sleepy dismal hollers
down the last hallway
where self-esteem peels
like paint from a vaulted ceiling
in a prison vestibule—
left only to brood
in the dark nooks
and crannies of their minds
doodling out their remaining days
cataloging clip-art and counting stars.

With fissures running through his world,
Charlie screamed:

The quiet revolution is upon us all
not in another hour but this hour...
prepare to paint your storm doors
the wrong shade of brown.

Prepositions

We gave up
on the dishes
in hopes
they would go away
from neglect
but they stubbornly stayed
lingering on the counter
in sullen disobedience
causing us to start eating out.
But where is out?
When we are out
it doesn't feel out anymore
when dining inside
the same establishment
day after day
—in or out!
like opening up
a bottle of Primativo
as if it needs to express itself more—
become assertive among extroverts!
plus the pressure of having to choose
between intro and extra
as if one cannot exist in between.
All these prepositions trouble me
inside my mind,
especially
when I'm under the weather...

Three Deadly Words

Hard for an aging poet to know
which words are out of vogue

Like moist—

Raised in the sixties you loved moist
as any kid dashing home from school
to sample newly baked Duncan Hines extra-moist
double-dutch chocolate brownies would tell you

But not now!
As I've been so politely informed by my daughter
wishing to save me from public embarrassment
lest I utter one of the seven words you cannot say in public

Like clown—

Well … you can say clown
if you are speaking metaphorically about an idiot
but not as a reference to a mime
who perchance is canvassing a quiet suburb in late October

Reminds me of a woebegone mime
I espied in Barcelona last summer
—nostalgic for the days
of Marcel Marceau, Red Skelton, and Emmet Kelly

Some words change slowly
as if time
allows us to see
their transmogrification

Like trump—

Once bestowing upon the card holder
confidence while playing pinochle
now the urban dictionary
informs me that trump means:

    ~ to compulsively lie
    ~ to be obsessively obscene
    ~ a fake or a fraud
    ~ hypocritical and lacking in self-control

Oh, generation weep
for the days of George Carlin
'suppose he knew quite well
that the seven words you cannot say in public

would someday become common,
replaced by new vulgarities
too repugnant to be uttered in any self-respecting company
like moist cake in the hand of a clown named trump

Terra Nova in Tirana

Boone barked nouns
signaling the neighbors
fractious cats
caterwauling adverbs
while the local rooster's
cockcrow
punctuated my covetous morning
censuring my sleep.

Devocalize the rooster!
Monastasize the cats!
And feed the newfie,
       whilst wondering…

> *now that Siri*
> *sets my alarm*
> *and draws the shades*
> *and reminds me*
> *where I stored the dog food,*
> *why hasn't Apple*
> *programmed a rooster*
> *with muted crows?*

I imagine Siri responding
       "frankly, I'm wondering that myself"
prompting an ill-fated loop
ending with more wondering
how this particular rooster
survived past
prime basting age

> *could he ever be a pet*
> *like my nouning newfie*
> *or those maddingly*
> *adverbing cats next door?*

Cats aren't generally annoying,
just those that choose
to live in the world
of incessant adverbs.

My Blue, curiously
devoid of elocution
precariously perches like a preposition
between the window
and the aquarium
one eye leering a Bolivian Pacu
immersed in another world.
Blue's gaze floating strangely,
perhaps wondering…

> *how this particular Pacu*
> *survived beyond*
> *prime basting age,*
> *could he ever be a friend*
> *like the neighbors adverbial cats*
> *or that damn nouning newfie?*

North Ontario

Tiny pictures flickerin'
pixels on a screen,
old man's far away from home
livin' in between
I hear you got older
all I got is dreams
and tiny pictures.

I hear the miners
are doin' fine,
diggin' gold and killin' time
in the mudville nine
But the dusk is fallin'
and a chill is in the air
only tiny pictures in my head

I got lost
in the misty mountains,
french horns moanin'
all over again
I feel like goin' back
to start all over
traveling light with tiny pictures

Well all those nights
and flat-screen avatars,
deep terabyte cellar
door to nowhere
I'll see you soon
draw a blue moon
upon your eyes
tiny pictures flickerin'
pixels inside a dream.

The Mountain That Eats Men

*The wretched of the earth do not decide to become extinct,
they resolve, on the contrary, to multiply:
life is their weapon against life, life is all that they have.*

—James Baldwin

*He hews out channels through the rocks, And his eye
sees anything precious.*

—Job 28:10

Precious!

—Gollum, Lord of the Rings

Part I: Pachamama

Pachamama was a silver spiral, winding
    to the heart of the mountain
    ascending and descending stairs
    from the Southern Cross to the stars of Orion
Pachamama, the sustainer of life
    once harvesting abundance
    she nourished us in this space
Pachamama was the giver of all things
    mediator, judge, maintainer of balance
    she testified to one single being
    the moon, stars, and a breathing universe.

Pachamama was kind—
    before conquistadors
        gobbled up slaves like sardines
Aymara and Quechua,
    Chiquitano, Guaraní, and Moxeño
    enslaved miners feeding globalistic cells
    human flotsam and jetsam
    sacrificed on the altar of progress
Replaced like broken farm equipment
    with one million more extracted
    from the heart of darkness
Life-sustaining catalysts
    metabolizing Western civilization
        nourishing the wealth of the wealthiest
        brazenly gorging on her innards
        like a midnight bazaar
From her depths, Pachamama testifies…
    when there is nothing left
        the expendable are left behind.

Part II: Potosi

I am rich Potosi,
treasure of the world.
the king of all mountains,
and the envy of all kings.
—Potosi coat of arms, late 16th century

Potosi, first city of capitalism,
    became sick with display and extravagance
    attracting artists, academics, priests, and prostitutes
Wealth flowed like water
    drained from 5,000 drifts
        bored from her veins
            for the fruit of her entrails
Now only vague memories of splendor

Gone the ladies sparkling in pearls,
    parading through salons
    boasting the finest tapestries
Gone the laces of Lille and Florentine brocades,
    the titled bore at bullfights,
    fiestas and masked balls
Gone the diamond-encrusted caballeros shields,
    gaudily plumed helmets
    and richly caparisoned ponies
Gone the church altars
    sparkling with silver filigree, where
    Dominicans, Franciscans, and Jesuits
    competed to save souls
    and stash pieces of eight

Behind the facade of progress lies the oldest story
    of exploitation and blighted lives,
        as the caballeros escaped with the shield
            we are left to dig for the dregs.

Part III: Peones

There are no trees
    on the mountain that eats men,
    only scattered eruptions of scrubby brush
Thin lines of smoke
    uncoiling from distant fires
    from shanty huts carved of her side
Sumaj Orko, beautiful hill
    once tall, proud perfect cone
    of slender form and reddish hues
Now summit lowered and landscape scarred
    rusting equipment and pathways
    pockmark her face
Ruinous landscape of slag and shavings
    noxious mounds of contaminants
    and open wounds remain
From speared sides gush springs
    seeping through a crazy quilt of garbage,
        watering eyes that quench the miner's thirst
        as they descend rickety ladders
        silently sifting their way
        through craggy holes
        and deep labyrinthian veins
    1,000 meters from the mouth of the grave
    where they are invisible
        and darkness is absolute.

I live
> between the hot tunnels of the mine
> and the chilly Altiplano winds
> in a tumbleweed neighborhood
>> called Calvary.

In our stone hut
> near an entrance to a tunnel
> mother sits drying our clothes
>> above a small fire
>>> that leaps from a tin can
>>> and the first sounds of the morning
>>>> are hammers against the ore

I work the bowels
> of Cerro Rico by night,
> compete for eco tourists'
>> short change by day
>> while luxury SUVs roll down
>>> the narrow, dusty streets

Peones like me are dust grains
> in the tunnels of Cerro Rico
> forever dreaming of a better life
> like our papis,
>> like their papis before.

The mountain is our identity
> and as the sinkholes begin to swallow
> and sinkholes scar her flanks
>> her mutilations become part of yourself
> mining hollow feelings
>> of an early grave.

Part III: El Tio

Down here, El Tio is lord of the earthen mine
    banished to the underworld's filthy heart
    no longer Lucifer but our Uncle
    skirting in the dark
Arbiter of fortune and death
    bulging eyes lord darkness from scarred clefts
    where good luck doesn't even fall in a fine drizzle
    but floats like fumes from a mercury dream
Down here, in this lamp-lit world
    no one seeks the aid of heaven
        no sermons, saints, or sages can protect
        while fitting dynamite in lonely holes.
Ay me, sad lonely Tio
    dressed in lights and dreams
        prefers the company of nobodies
    who do not have names but numbers.
Down here, Uncle is always hungry
        every night's a last supper
    of cigarettes and coca leaves
    and sacramental el puro served at the shrine.

Papi said a miner must have faith,
    but we play a double faith.
    Inside the mine
    I believe Tio will save me,
    outside I pray to the Virgin Mary
    to save Papi
        from lung cancer, mal de mina
save Papi, from sniffing-glue headaches
save Papi, from systemic poisoning
        losing teeth and bleeding gums
        losing hearing from ruptured eardrums
only alcohol and coca leaves ease the pain

Rise eat drill blast haul
rise eat drill blast haul
this is the miner's birthright
    to eke out a life
        amidst the toxic gasses
            in the devil's lair.
Uncle Tio giveth,
    and Uncle Tio taketh away.

Papi died last week
    from silicosis at thirty-five,
        the miner's birthright
And I am left
    with a bitter taste.

Part IV: Testimonial

Nobody will put walls to our truth.
Evil never lasted a hundred years nor were there people who resist.

—Nilo Soruco, La Caraqueña

Today, Pachamama is hollow
Por Soledad!
    she has not once slept these past 500 years
    whilst men gorged themselves
    relentlessly on her breasts
Pachamama testifies: conquistadors never left
    as gold and silver gave way
        to lithium, tantalum, and palladium
They assumed new names
    like Sumitomo, Pan American, Glencore,
    and Coeur d'Alene
        with no more interest
           in setting laborer's free
                than cleaning the arsenic-laced Río Pilcomayo.

Let us enter her hallowed womb
    to listen while she trembles—

    Look up, and see the moon
        shedding tears of silver
        upon the earth's driest indifference
    Look down, stones do not offend
        silver covets nothing
        metals are not reborn, nor do they grow anew
    Look now, this poison
        penetrates to the marrow
        awaken, there is no tomorrow.

As we grope in caverns dark
    where neither seraphim nor raindrops go,
    who will march for Pachamama
    before the echoes fade below?
In the end,
    who will testify
    to the mountain that eat men
    this abattoir, our miner's home?

www.ingramcontent.com/pod-product-compliance
Lightning Source LLC
LaVergne TN
LVHW010035070426
835507LV00006B/144